RSAC

DEC 1997

THE ANDREW POEMS

THE ANDREW POEMS

by Shelly Wagner

Texas Tech University Press

This book was set in Caslon and printed on acid-free paper that meets the guidelines for permanence and durability of the Committee on Production Guidelines for Book Longevity of the Council on Library Resources.

Jacket design by Kerri Carter.

Printed in the United States of America.

Library of Congress Cataloging-in-Publication Data
Wagner, Shelly.
    The Andrew poems / by Shelly Wagner.
       p. cm.
    ISBN 0-89672-319-4 (cloth).
       1. Parent and child—Poetry. 2. Children—Death—Poetry.
I. Title.
PS3573.A3872A53 1994
813'.54—dc20   93-17769
                                                             CIP

    96 97 98 99 00 01 02 / 9 8 7 6

Texas Tech University Press
Lubbock, Texas 79409-1037 USA

Grateful acknowledgment is made to the editors of the following publications where these poems, sometimes in different form, first appeared:

American Poetry Review: "Blackbirds," "The Boxes," "Gorillas," "Television"
Bluff City: "Birth of a Child," "Home"
Hampden-Sydney Poetry Review: "A Happy Poem," "Wet"
ONTHEBUS: "Ashley," "The Limousine," "Passover," "Rusty," "Shoes," "The Tie," "Voices"
Poetry East: "Foxes," "The Gold Sofa," "The Grocery Store," "The Pearl"
TriQuarterly: "Thomas's Birthday," "Treasure," "What If"
The Virginian-Pilot: "Communion," "I Thirst"

Preface

What an awesome and wonderful book this is, a sustained and poignant cycle of poems I doubt I'll ever find equalled. This woman has looked into her heart and written with grace, without flinching. Reading *The Andrew Poems*, I believe we can look into our own hearts and begin being healed.

Judith Keeling, Editor of the Texas Tech University Press, always holds me to one absolute standard for any book I recommend: "Must we publish this book?" When I finished *The Andrew Poems*, the first summary words I scribbled were these: "Stunning; beautiful; terrible and sad; human and necessary. We must publish this."

When I recommended the book to her, I wrote, "Before you read it, though, fasten your seat belt, and pray that your air bag works: you're in for a head-on collision with grief." *The Andrew Poems* is joy and sorrow and love turned into poetry after the worst loss possible, the death of one's own child.

Literary history is shot through with moving poems on this subject, but I've never seen such a sustained outpouring of poetry on loss—successful, moving poems—as this book by Shelly Wagner. I think of *Kindertotenlieder*—"Songs on the Deaths of Infants." "Controlled heartbreak," author Joy Williams called it.

Matthew Arnold spoke of great literary passages as "touchstones" by which we can measure the power and beauty of contemporary poems. Literature gives us ample moments of such "terrible beauty," poems on the death of children—e.g., King David's lament for his son Absalom, and recent poems by Ben Jonson, Jon Silkin, Michael S. Harper.

Sometimes, a poet's strategy in trying to deal with the intense grief and pain is to deny, to altogether avoid risking sentimentality—for example, the urgent poem by Dylan Thomas called "A Refusal to Mourn the Death of a Child, by Fire, in London," and John Crowe Ransom's "Bells for John Whiteside's Daughter."

I've read hundreds, even thousands, of sincere, painful verses that are touching statements of grief, but seem less successful as poems. Everyone suffers many, many losses in a lifetime; as poet John Biguenet wrote, "Everyone begs for mercy." If someone has children and hasn't had to write about the loss of a child, chances are good that she or he has written poems dreading a child's death, aware of risks and the fragile bubble of our lives.

After years of reading such poems—and as a father and grandfather—I'm both jaded about and vulnerable to the subject. I was drawn to Shelly Wagner's book by the power of the poems themselves, even more than by the distressing subject matter. I kept asking myself, "Who has turned the loss of a child into *poems* as powerfully as Shelly Wagner has, in *The Andrew Poems*?" I can't recall any book that matches hers.

Examples of how excellent I find this book? See as examples "Treasure," "Gorillas," "The Boxes," "Television," "Thomas's Birthday," "In Our Beds," "Again," "Looking for Myself," "My Husband," "In the Taxi," "The Dance," "Your Questions," "Thirteenth Birthday," "Driving," "What If?" and "My Work."

What drew me to Shelly Wagner's poems in journals were the beauty of sounds and stunning discoveries building to bold and heart-breaking closure. Her poems are grounded in vivid, sensuous details, which alone can make rich poetry. Sounds are another recurring strong point; read those poems aloud, if you can, and hear them. Her metaphors and similes also stun me time after time, and her vivid images—painful, shockingly beautiful ways of sharing the old concerns. Closure is for me the final test of whether a poem is ripe, whether a poet is consistently skillful. Consider the closure of any of the poems listed above.

As no other has ever done, this book makes me feel part of the struggling, lovely human tribe. Her poems make me think of John Donne's famous Devotion:

No man is an island, entire of itself; every man is a piece of
the continent, a part of the main; if a clod be washed away by
the sea, Europe is the less. . . ; any man's death diminishes me,
because I am involved in mankind; and therefore never send to know
for whom the bell tolls; it tolls for thee.

I urged Judith to fasten her seat belt. One after another, though, Shelly Wagner's poems reach out and unstrap us; we're forced head-on into the pathos, the overwhelming beauty, the sense of unbearable loss. And as we read on, the only cushioning restraints are the beauty of language, the aesthetic and emotional impact of poetry (which intensify feelings even more, of course).

What saves us, then, as readers? How can we bear it? Why should we try to cope with such loss, until we might have to? If Aristotle was right, a drama like this arouses our pity and fear: compassion, as we empathize; and fear, as we identify with and realize that the grief overwhelming the characters might happen also to us.

Aristotle spoke of catharsis, the purging of troubling emotions. Whether literature works exactly that way or not, I believe that feeling such terrible beauty deeply for a while is what we find in great stories and plays and poems.

As if thinking of Aristotle, Wagner has determined in these poems:

to speak the unspeakable,
recapture in foolish, shallow syllables
the trauma of loss
so you might
know for a moment
grief that gives life,
transcends,
blesses with wisdom.
("Your Questions," stanza one)

It is no easy fix she gives us. How can we bear it? Some may barely be able to try, and so she writes a happy poem at her other son's request about her rose garden, even though "the garden is the size and shape / of our family plot at the cemetery." For his sake, though, she decides to "change / the names of the roses to suit myself / and this poem."

> I'll invite strangers
> to walk through the liquid aroma,
> to dangle their feet in my fountain of youth.
> I'll ask them to stretch out their hands,
>   touch the petals
> like Adam reaching for the finger of God.
>   ("A Happy Poem")

Patiently, in the spirit of the healing purging of disturbing emotions, she continues:

> It's your choice to not listen
> if you cannot bear
> what I also thought
> I could not survive.
> I will understand
> and wait
> until you need this lesson
> like a lifeline
> when you are drowning.
> You will die, too, you know.
> There's nothing I can do about it
> but have you drown in my poem
> for only a moment,
> then come gulping to the surface
> looking into my eyes
> smiling because you are not dead
> but happier than you were before
> to shake the water off your head,
> go home and kiss your children,
> tuck them in bed,
> sleep yourself unsettled
> but wake somehow refreshed.
>   ("Your Questions," stanza one)

"Fear death by drowning," T.S. Eliot wrote. In *Lord Jim*, Joseph Conrad has Stein give this advice about coping, in spite of the fear of death (by water): "to the destructive element submit yourself, and with the exertions of your hands and feet in the water make the deep, deep sea keep you up."

The dangerous element: yes, that's what this book offers, and a hauntingly beautiful way of coping. One of James Dickey's best books of poems is *Drowning with Others*. Wagner's book is like that, and might have been titled that. Her book makes us feel the cost of the joy and pain of being human and suffering loss and turning heartbreak into elegy.

Other sole survivors of drowning in literature come back to tell us disturbing stories—for example, Ishmael, in *Moby Dick* ("Call me Ishmael," he says as he begins his tale); and the narrator of Coleridge's "Rime of the Ancient Mariner," who stops one wedding guest out of three and tells his obsessive tale.

"So I keep telling my story," Wagner concludes stanza one of "Your Questions." And what she tells compels us.

> Do not avoid my eyes.
> Do not walk away from me.
> I am a mother.
> Come close, sit down
> and listen.
> ("Your Questions," stanza two)

This is so much more than simply a collection of poems; key words and images recur, building on each other, relentlessly telling the story of Andrew and a mother's love—more than we expected to know, almost more loss and beauty than we can bear.

Miller Williams said it, in his poem about how to write poetry, "Let Me Tell You": do all you can do to find a good line, he advised; the person you grieve for

> will forgive you
> if the line you found was a good line.
>
> It does not have to be worth the dying.

Walter McDonald
Series Editor

Contents

THE ANDREW POEMS

for Thomas

Treasure

Follow my hand into this trunk.
Examine for yourself its treasure.
Lift and read the heavy wooden board,
a scrap of lumber
on which he scrawled his name—
red letters, all capitals,
the E backwards.
In kindergarten he learned
to sign perfectly his many drawings,
the jewels of his last will and testament.
Try on his brilliant yellow sunglasses.
See the world as he saw it—clearly
full of hope.
Slide your hand up the sleeve
of his favorite red shirt
as though you were to tickle him.
He would laugh. You may cry.
Finally, with utmost care,
hold what he made in nursery school—
a white plaster cast of his hand,
fingers spread wide apart
as though he were telling you
how old he would be when he died.

Birth of a Child

The birth began with a silent splash,
my womb weeping.
The crown of the baby's head
opened my body
like a camera lens
photographing the end of our union.
A doctor's hands
as large as the child's torso
freed the right shoulder,
then the left,
allowing the wet, slippery little boy
to appear.
The child was laid like a gift on my breast.
Our hearts' duet continued.
My heart would not stop
pumping our blood
through the thick blue braid of veins,
its pulse pounded like a fist
to protest sterile scissors
cutting our connection.

Mice

A life parallel
behind our refrigerator—
a mother raising her two baby mice.
Her children played where they shouldn't.
I could hear her scream in her squeaky voice
as her babies ran fearlessly
across our kitchen floor.

Thomas, my nine-year-old man-
of-the-house, set the trap with cheese.
Three-year-old Andrew wandered in
as we lay the loaded trap on the floor;
I perched him on the kitchen counter
with the impossible command,
"Do not move."
Thomas and I armed ourselves
with a mop and a broom
and jumped up on the ledge with Andrew.

The babies, weighing less than
your last breath,
sashayed down the alley
between the refrigerator and cabinet.
Like children on a jungle gym,
they climbed over the locking bar,
slipped across the spring,
ate the orange cheese.
When they heard us laughing
the mice jumped off

as though sliding from Santa's knee,
too small to trip the trap,
too young to know the danger.

Andrew went to his room,
returned with his toys.
He parked two Matchbox cars
in front of the refrigerator,
set up a tiny picnic table
with two chairs and an umbrella,
then set the table with cheese.
He waited until he had to go to bed.

While Andrew and Thomas slept
I ate the cheese
the way I ate
Santa's cookies and milk.
I never told the boys
that during the night
the trap killed the mother,
and her two babies
would not survive.

Passover

The passover posts and lintels
were not more clearly marked
than our back door
the afternoon you butchered
your package of school photos
with blunt kindergarten scissors
and taped thirty-six wallet-size pictures
up and down the frame
around the kitchen door,
completing your ceremony
with the ultimate sacrifice—
your eight-by-tens and five-by-sevens
hung on the wooden door.
In dismantling your shrine,
removing the photos of my lamb,
was I oblivious as the pharaoh
to the significance of this act?
Had your statement of faith
remained on our door,
would the Angel of Death have passed over?

Gorillas

I found the gorilla mask in the closet.
I was not looking for it.
Holding the limp, black rubber head
covered with coarse hair,
I remembered your blue eyes
peering through its empty sockets.
We had bought it for Halloween
but it came to life
the day you wore it to the zoo.
The huge head almost covered your shoulders.
You kept poking your fingers into the holes
to keep them in front of your eyes
so you could see to lead me

to the huge gorilla.
He stopped pacing and fixed his gorilla eyes
on the little monkey approaching.
He found you irresistible.
His arms opened wide.
He grasped the bars and began to sway
side to side, staring at you.
You stood at the fence outside his cage
mimicking him.
The two of you were dancing—
him leading, you following,

you leading, him following.
Two gorillas, two children
ignoring the crowd gathering.

It was a glorious afternoon,
the kind only a child
can give a parent and a gorilla.
As we were walking away
I looked back at the animal.
He was pathetic trapped in his cage,
his chest pressed against the bars,
his arms reaching through
as though he knew
he would never see you again.
Now all I have
is this memory
and this mask
lying collapsed in my lap
as though the life has gone out of it
and it has begun slowly to decompose.

The Boxes

When I told the police I couldn't find you,
they began a search that included everything,
even the boxes in the house:
the footlockers of clothes in the attic,
the hamper in the bathroom,
the Chinese lacquered trunk by the sofa.
They made me raise every lid.
I told them you would never stay in a box,
not with all the commotion.
You would have jumped out,
found your flashlight
and wanted to join the search.

Poor Thomas, leading men
who didn't know us
through neighbors' garages
where you never played,
hoping they were right
and we were wrong
and he would find you
and snatch you home by the hand

so the police cars would
get out of our driveway
and the divers would
get out of our river

because it was certainly
past our bedtime.
We would double-bolt our doors
like always,
say longer prayers than usual.
I could have put my children to bed.
But during the night
I would have sat until morning
beside my sleeping boys.

That's not what happened.
Thomas is still here, now older.
I still go to his room
when he is sleeping
just to look at him.
I still visit the cemetery,
not as often,
but the urge is the same:
to lie down on the grass,
put my arm around the hump of ground
and tell you, "Get out of this box!
Put a stop to this commotion. Come home.
You should be in bed."

Wet

Near midnight,
your grandfather came into your room
where Thomas and I had waited.
He said you had been found
and they needed something to cover you,
not for the cold—it was summer,
not for your comfort—too late;
but to wrap the small, wet body
as with a shroud.
I grabbed your bedspread,
gave it to your grandfather.
He left your room
carrying your white spread
draped in his arms
like a child.

I'd rather remember you
wet from your bath.
You would play until chilled and wrinkled.
Then I would wrap
a thick white towel around you.
We loved the patting,
tickling, laughing,
and dusting with powder.
After you wiggled into your pajamas
you would climb on the hamper
to see yourself in the mirror,
comb your wet hair straight back

and ask
if that made you look famous?
With affirmations,
I would carry my legend to his room.

Had I gone outside that night,
no one would have let me bathe you,
wash the mud from your cheeks and legs.
What good to dry and powder you?
You could not come back to your room.
But I wonder,
did the river sweep your wet hair straight back
and make you famous?

Television

He watched the soaps at lunch,
eating peanut butter and jelly
at the coffee table
with his grandmother
and "The Young and the Restless."
He couldn't play "Wheel of Fortune,"
but he loved Vanna White.
We competed for his affection.
She had something I didn't have—
he was crazy about her letters.
"The Price Is Right"
was his favorite.
If I wanted him
to come in from the yard
or from his room to the kitchen,
all I had to do was call,
"Andrew Minton! Come on down!"
One day, racing down our hall
in response to the silly summons,
he leapt into my arms,
clasped my face between his hands,
held me steady,
and planted a huge smooch
right on my lips,
his head moving side to side
like those bobbing dogs

in the rear windows of cars.
"Andrew, my goodness!"
He hopped down explaining,
"That's how they do it
on the 'Young and the Restless.'"

The day we were to bury him
I stood at my closet,
reached for my black dress
with the big white collar
and inappropriate white polka dots.
I know one doesn't wear polka dots
to a funeral
but the Sunday before,
he beamed when he saw me,
"Mom, you look like
'The Young and the Restless.'"
Vanna did not come to his funeral.
She does not know she has lost a fan.
That day
after everyone was gone
I walked to the river.
Standing there in my polka dots,
I looked up at the sky
as one does when addressing the dead,
"Andrew Minton, come on down."

The Limousine

When the burial was over,
I turned away from the mourners
and your new grave
and through a door held open for me,
stepped into the black limousine.
Quietly the car moved along,
leaving at the cemetery
the other funeral car:
your empty hearse
parked at your grave,
its rear door still wide open.
Proceeding at a slow speed,
dark windows insulated me
from traffic, shoppers, businesses
open as usual.
The world looked like
an old black-and-white movie
I couldn't recall.
People stopped to watch the limousine pass.
Perhaps some glimpsed
the woman's face
framed in the window.
Could they see
in this portrait of a mother
she would live for years
enclosed in this long, black car?

Thomas's Birthday

You drowned on Thursday.
We buried you on Saturday.
Your brother's birthday was Sunday.
We didn't need food.
Friends had filled our home
with deviled eggs, fried chicken,
cold cuts, cooked hams. You would have loved
our stuffed refrigerator,
its door still sporting your drawings.
Someone brought a cake
with twelve candles.
We circled the kitchen table.
Your brother smiled bravely;
thanked everyone for their gifts,
including the brightly striped beach chair
with a matching towel.
For a moment Thomas tried
to amuse us.
He wrapped the colored towel
around his shoulders
and sat in his striped chair.
He was a sight. Some laughed.
But to me it looked like Joseph's coat
of many colors—proof that a son was dead.
I left
to find the sparklers
we had saved from the fourth of July.
I put one on the cake,
lit it,
we all sang.
The sparkler burned and exploded
until it was a charred black stick
crumpled in the center of the cake

filling the kitchen with smoky incense.
Someone was worried it would
burn down the house.
Who cares?
We lit the candles.
Thomas looked my way,
took my hand,
made a wish
and blew out all the flames.
Suddenly it seemed the three of us were alone
in our backyard:
me lying on the ground—
another drowning victim,
Thomas kneeling over me
covering my mouth with his,
steadily blowing into me,
and you
pacing back and forth on the water
crying to him,
"Save her! Save her!"

The Pearl

Never saying goodbye,
I return over and over
to sit on the dirt mattress
covered with the bright green grass blanket
made from seed sewn by your grandfather.
Unlike the mother and child we once were,
you have gone without my permission,
not holding my hand,
through a door I cannot open.
At the grave,
you are now the wiser one
but death will not let you
give me answers.
And would I believe you if you said,
"The pain that has come between us
will someday be our pearl?"

Ashley

His six-year-old girlfriend
walked up our lane
carrying too much sorrow
and her gift—
a small glass jar
full of miniature shells,
tiny baby conchs,
a hole in each one
like a jar full of pearls.
She came when I was suffering.
She climbed into bed with me,
under the covers
the way Andrew used to do.
She began to weep
so we poured out the shells
and counted them.
For each one
we shared a memory.
We took turns
the way one does with children.
I remember planning
to string the shells one day
and wear them in tribute to Andrew.
I never did.
They are a tribute to her,
still in the jar
with the red-checked lid.

Blackbirds

The birds came to pay their respects
when the trees were bare.
Hundreds of huge blackbirds
filled our oak with their bodies.
The tree turned black
as though observing
the old funeral custom
of being draped in crape.
Suddenly, the sign of mourning was lifted
as the birds took flight in unison.
Then they began to land on the ground,
at first, only a few.
The blackness spread
as each bird landed beside another.
It appeared as a cloth
unrolled across the lawn.
The gesture complete,
they lifted the veil and were gone.

The Grocery Store

It seemed sacrilegious
to shop for groceries so soon after the funeral.
But there was no milk, no bread
and no, I couldn't let others
shop for Thomas and me.

I would get up.
Dress—but not like I used to.
Brush my hair—but not like I used to.
Go to the store, avoid the cereal aisle
with its colorful boxes, sugar and prizes—
not like I used to.

I had everything on my list
when reaching for the milk,
I saw the cream cheese—
cream cheese with green pepper jelly—
your favorite.
You'd clumsily smother it on crackers,
loving it more than guests.

Dashing for the shortest line,
I dropped my things next to hers,
her eggs, milk, bread, and two tomatoes.
She was so tiny—

proof that we shrink with age.
Our eggs side by side
but forty years at least between us.
How would I survive forty years?

I listened as she gently instructed the young man.
She said she lived on the second floor.
Would he please put her things in two bags?
"Don't bruise the lovely tomatoes. Put them on top.
Would you double-bag the eggs? Put them on top."
Pleased, she paid and picked up her groceries.
I watched her walk away.
The automatic doors opened as though in respect for her
as she carried her perishables balanced in two bags.

Shoes

After the death of my child,
I believed it possible
that clothing, toys, rooms,
even shoes
could become shrines.
I carried his little pairs of shoes
full of holes and memories
to the trash.
Hearing the garbage truck coming,
I made myself go inside
but I stood at the window to watch
as the contents of the can
were tossed into the truck.
Those men did not know
what I knew
before they drove away:
I had made a mistake.
I wanted to chase them,
stop them,
get back my baby's shoes.
For weeks I had nightmares.
I dreamed of going to the dump
to search for them,
dig for them,

find them
and bring them home.
The shoes are gone—

but not all of them.
Andrew, I kept my favorites:
the chalk-white tennis shoes
you polished the night before
with baby shoe polish,
your favorite checkerboard slip-ons,
my favorite teddy bear slippers
and your reliable red rubber boots.
I wish I had your loafers
with your lucky pennies in them.
You were buried wearing those.
Today, the shoes
are lined up in pairs
like left-facing and right-facing griffins
on guard under your mother's bed.

The Tie

At night, I imagine
lying on my side next to him,
my arm under his head,
whispering in his ear,
smoothing the child-sized red tie
that lies on his chest
like an upside-down
exclamation mark.
I put off buying him
men's clothing,
but for Easter
he wanted a tie—
a red one
and a navy blue blazer.
Now, just under six years old,
he is buried
wearing it forever—
as old a man
as he will ever be.
At night,
lying next to my husband,
I back into
the curved question mark
of his body
and ask,
"What is Andrew like now?"
He always whispers,
"His coat and tie are the same."

Faded

After the funeral
I went to the cemetery
and pulled each blossom off its stem
the way you picked flowers,
bringing me a bouquet
cupped in the palm of your hand.
I left at the grave
wreaths of barren stems,
then buried the dining room table
with petals,
trying to dry them, preserve them.
I still have them
but they are faded.

Your uncle framed six of your drawings,
the smiling clowns with your trademark eyelashes:
straight lines with tiny circles on each tip.
You used every magic marker,
each eyelash was a different hue.
They were vibrant, but he hung your pictures
near a window. The lashes and smiles
disappeared in the sunlight.

Your brother and I noticed
every blond little boy.
It was a game we played:
looking for hair like yours,
a head shaped like yours,
anything like yours

but I knew the game was over
when he asked,
"Mom, when you close your eyes,
can you still see him?"

Someone offering comfort said,
"This will pass."
I recoiled like a slapped child,
fearing if the grief were to fade,
I would be left with nothing.

Voices

In the next dressing room
I hear a mother and child.

The child has no use for shopping.
He pleads with his mother,

"Pick me up, Mom. Pick me up."
I hear you calling me from the river bed,

"Pick me up, Mom. Pick me up."
The child next door persists,

"Please, Mom, please."
"Please, Mom, please," you echo.

The voices run me out of the dressing room
to my mother waiting in the store.

"Mom, get me out of here," I cry.
"Mom, get me out of here," I hear.

Our Song

My memory is a divining rod.
It finds us near water:
late afternoon by the ocean,
our last summer,
just the two of us on the beach.
As though cutting a record,
you track in circles around me
dragging a stick in the sand,
leaving groove after groove
surrounding my chair.
I play and replay the recording
with eyes shut,
head bent over,
fingertips drumming
the arm of my rocker.
Listening to our song,
I don't care the needle is stuck
while I *grieve, grieve, grieve.*

Rusty

She can hear her sons' gentle golden retriever,
the only witness to the drowning,
sighing outside her closed bedroom door.
His toenails click against the hardwood floor
as he crosses his heavy paws
under his greying chin.
Like a stone lion
by steps leading into a museum,
he settles beside her door.
He will wait for the grieving mother.
She will not come out for a very long time.
She is gazing at portraits of her son
hung on the walls of her mind.

Home

I live here
watching over and over
the movie of our life
playing on white plaster walls.
Handprints on woodwork wave
as I walk by.
Rooms laugh.
Floors run toward me at bedtime.
His pillow prays,
"If I should die
before I wake . . .."
Rain taps on his windowpane
like children
wanting him to play—
but it's too late.
I lie down
beside the bulkhead,
pull the river up
around my ears
and listen
to the crabs tell me
how natural he looked,
how peaceful,
as though he were only sleeping.

Communion

On the first anniversary of your death,
I went to the kitchen,
set the table with your Superman place mat
and pulled up your chair.
I made a peanut butter and jelly sandwich,
removed the crust as always
for a special occasion.
I cut it into quarters
and arranged the triangles
on your red plate.
I poured milk in your blue plastic
Crayola crayon mug,
put on its pointed top
with the hole in the tip for a straw.
I had no straws.
I don't buy them anymore.
Sitting next to your place,
I apologized for no straw.
I apologized for your death.
I apologized for not being there.
When I finished,
I wiped my eyes with your napkin,
gave thanks,
ate the bread and drank the milk.

My Garden

The ground beneath his tire swing
was scraped bare—
there was the beginning
of my garden.
His brother climbed the tree
and cut the rope.
I cut down the tree.
We hung the tire
on the wall in the garage
like an athlete's retired jersey.
Along the fence we dug a huge bed.
I planted azaleas called "Mother's Day,"
bleeding hearts,
Easter lilies—the resurrection flower.
I tried to grow *Gypsophila*,
known as baby's breath,
but it has not survived.
Golden jonquils trumpet
they are coming back.
My irises
are deep blue
like his eyes.
There's lots of yellow
coreopsis—he was a blond.
I checked this morning
for the tulips.
They are breaking the surface

looking for me.
Do you see my garden?
Do you see my madness:
blue eyes, blond hair,
two lips breaking
the surface
looking for me?

Andrew and Thomas

A simple question,
Never a problem before.
"Do you have any children?"
Really a simple question.
Easy. I say, "Yes," but
What do I say to "How many?"

"Two," my hard-headed
Heart always says.
One is dead.
Must I say only one?
Absolutely not—I have two
Sons.

White Ducks

White ducks lay in our yard like a pond
of spilled milk.
Thomas, my dark-haired child,
approached the ducks reservedly,
parting them like white foam on the Red Sea.
Andrew, my blond child,
arms waving wildly,
ran with abandon into their midst.
In a second they were gone.

We're told to cast our bread upon the waters.
I'll fill the river with crumbs
and cover the lawn like manna.
The ducks will come back,
lift as they did for Andrew,
show his mother what it looks like
when the spirit rises from the body.

Dust

My mother visits, brings dinner,
checks the house for ghosts.
She finds them hunkered down in corners—
amorphous, harmless fluff
avoiding the broom
she swings through the house
like a scythe.
She does not find humorous
the notes I leave at night
written in all capitals
on dark table tops,
"DUST ME."
"You cannot live like this," she says.
But I don't mind the company
of dust. My home is open
to hordes of specs that dance in sunlight.
When death empties a house,
cobwebs growing in thresholds
are welcome signs of life.

My Father

He can fix anything.
Yesterday he mended the broken beak of a shorebird
carved ten years ago for me.
Not since Andrew died
has he carved a block of wood.
For years Dad freed birds
trapped in tupelo and bass.
Andrew's task was to name them
Big Bird, Bert and *Ernie*.
At his grandfather's right hand,
Andrew watched rows of feathers
burned into ducks' backs,
glass eyes set in small heads,
iridescent colors painted on wings,
flight feathers glued on a pintail, one at a time.

One summer night, long after Andrew's bedtime,
I found them outside on the back porch
working on a duck under the bug light.
As though soothing the bird,
Dad was sanding its neck.
In rocking chairs facing the moon,
they did not see me—
Andrew barefoot in his baby-blue pajamas,
my father in his white cotton robe—
The blue glow from the bug light
covered them like first frost.
On that hot summer night, they looked cold—

ice sculpture
of grandfather and grandson.
I can still see the halo of my father's bald head
leaning toward Andrew's silky hair.
I can hear the zapping of the bug light,
bugs over their heads dying,
flying from the dark into the light.

The Gold Sofa

He wanted it to be a surprise—
the gold sofa from the Salvation Army.
During my last visit with my brother
I slept on a mattress on the floor.
"Please, come back for a week,
for a month," your uncle had urged.

There it was in front of his windows,
stretched out in the sun,
shaped like a long box,
longer than me lying down,
with three loose back pillows,
very worn.

It was on sale, half-price, ten dollars.
He had carried it across town
tied on top of his small car.
He and a neighbor had twisted it
up three flights,
the lower end on my brother's head.

He is at work now,
happy that I am comfortable—
and I am, surrounded by pillows,
sitting cross-legged, reading
in the corner of the sofa in the sun.
Sitting here, how odd to read my brother's poems
about your funeral.
I remember the funeral director saying,

"We have only two caskets for children.
They are four feet six inches long.
I know which one you will want."

There it was—closed—
in front of the church—
blue, handsome, shiny, cold.
But I had seen the velvet cushions
at the funeral home—
clean, soft, silver.
We put stuffed animals
and poems all around you—
you lying there in the box
just longer than you.

Keeping it level, six friends
carried the small casket
to the hearse.
We followed the long, black car
across town to the cemetery.
In the rain,
we buried you.

Folding my brother's poems like letters,
I wonder are you reading yours?
I lie down on my sofa.
How sweet of my brother
to buy this for me,
to carry it across town.
He did it because he loves me

so do not tell him
in a dream or a poem
that I am stretched out with all
one feels when her child dies,
arms folded across my chest,
eyes closed like two caskets,
lying at rigid attention
rehearsing the moment
we will be alike again.

In Our Beds

Midday,
I call a newly grieving mother.
She is in bed, her voice in pain.
She has come home
to an empty house—her young son
is dead.
"Coming home is hard," she says,
but where else can she go?
I remember days, weeks, months
in my bedroom
climbing vines in the wallpaper,
ripping off leaves,
pressing flowers
between pages of memory.
I'd climb to the top of the branches,
try to break through
to the other side.
Giving up,
I'd look down like God
at myself lying in the bed:
my hair a mess, my eyes bloodshot,
a white handkerchief in one hand,
my child's red shirt in the other,
a comforter
pulled tightly under my chin,
pillows around me like clouds.
I've heard of a woman,
an expert who writes about death,
who when weary lies on her bed
to allow six angels

to minister to her.
They stroke her forehead,
fingertips and toes.
She is refreshed. I've tried it,
but I've never seen six angels,
not even one. I've never felt them
touching me.
Perhaps
the key to this mystery
is the lying down to wait.

Again

A small thing can bring it all back.
A black thing can bring it all back.
A dog can bring it all back.
A small, black dog can bring it all back
if he is missing.
One night the dog did not come
when my brother called.
His dog doesn't know this yard.
Andrew did. He would play
along the concrete-bag bulkhead,
chase ducks from the lawn,
check crab pots at the pier,
swing near the river curled in his tire,
race down the hill in his blue wagon
in the summer,
race down the hill in his snow saucer
in the winter.
His whole short life racing
to its end at the river.
He is gone now and so is Black Dog.
Again
we search the neighborhood with flashlights.
Again,
no success.
Finally we give up,
come home, then my brother
finds him in the river behind the house

trapped by low tide—
a wet, scared dog
who could not climb the concrete bags.
Grabbing him by the scruff of his neck,
my brother yanks him up.
"I hope you've learned your lesson!
Bad dog."
He falls to his knees,
embraces the wet animal.
"Good boy."
Life is ironic,
even a happy ending.
Why couldn't the dog die
and Andrew live?
Why the high tide
when Andrew fell
and almost no water
when the dog falls?
Could we not sacrifice the dog
like an Old Testament lesson
and learn so the child
might be saved?
Must the child die
to save the mother?
Must one die for all?
Have we learned our lessons?

Looking for Myself

I no longer answer to my name.
You'll find me in the Old Testament.
I am Samson teasing fate.
I am Delilah teasing Samson.
My hair is long.
My hair is short.
I can see.
I am blind.
I am God against the Philistines.
I am Samson's hand against the column.
I am the force bringing down the temple.
I am the broken column.
I am a dead Philistine.
I am the empty socket of Sampson's eye.
In the New Testament, remember the prodigal son?
I am he.
I am his father.
I am his brother left behind.
I am his mother never mentioned.
I am the wealth he squanders.
I am the pigs he feeds.
I am the feed.
I am the leaving.
I am the returning.
I am the forgiven.
I am the forgiveness.

Three Weeks

I broke Andrew once. I did.
I thought he was in the kitchen.
I backed my car in the driveway
for Thomas to wash
and I ran over Andrew,
even pulled forward
and ran over him again,
thinking Thomas screamed
because a toy
was caught under the rear wheel.
It was not a toy—
"You broke me," he cried.
His thigh was sprung
like a wishbone.
We were lucky.
The bone would heal.

Three years old,
he lay in a hospital crib
three weeks.
I stayed with him,
my muscles as tense
as his thigh pulled in traction
allowing the broken bone to line up,
lay down new tissue,
bond, reconnect.
The first doctor used tape
to attach cords to his knee.
I could have told him
tape would never hold
my little boy.
The knee slipped out,

crashed to the bed.
A second doctor,
a second opinion:
a pin to be drilled through the knee,
traction cords tied
to either side
of a protruding stainless-steel pin.
That worked, but it hurt.
The doctor drilled
after shooting the knee
with novacaine.
Andrew felt the needles,
he felt the drill boring through the bone,
he cried; I cried.
It didn't take long;
in minutes the doctor was gone,
leaving me by my child's bed
pushing his hair off his forehead,
wiping tears from his cheeks,
rounding my mouth,
blowing on the wounds
around the pin through his knee.
Months later the bone was healed.
Years later I married the second doctor—
I told you the leg was a wishbone.

The days were long those three weeks;
days for me to nurse him,
bathe him,
read to him,
play with him,
just look at him.
I was lucky; he was lucky,

luckier than the little girl
in the next room.
She was Andrew's age
with Andrew's blond hair,
beautiful
but scarred for life.
Her mother
had sat her in boiling water—
punishment for wetting her bed.
Now she was cared for daily
by nurses.
She would remain when we went home—
more skin to graft,
scars to heal,
pain to endure,
all without her mother.

How lucky Andrew and I were.
How close we had come
to an accident
that would end it all.
Andrew would go home
in a full body cast.

Some children
never went home
like the twelve-year-old boy
who died of leukemia.
It was almost 9 PM—
late on the children's ward
when children and their parents
end another day of waiting
for bone to reconnect,

skin to graft,
drugs to work,
miracles to occur.
The night nurse came into our room
on cushioned white soles.
Without a word, she walked to our window
that looked into the hall,
dropped the blind
like a thin white veil.
She was entering and exiting every room,
sealing the corridor,
silently dividing the living
from the dead.
How many times
in turning the wands on our blinds
had she touched the mystery
that partitions life and death?
Slightly separating the slats,
I could see she had dimmed
the lights in the hall.
At windows across the corridor,
blinds parted
like squinting eyelids.
We all watched our young neighbor,
rolled by our windows on a gurney.
Forlorn shadows,
his family followed, weeping,
even the nurse—
but not his mother.
She walked beside him
still holding his hand.
I snatched my fingertips

from between the slats,
closing myself
and my lucky child
behind the blind.
Only the turn of a wand separated us
from the mother and child in the hall.

You know our story—
wishbones are temporary.
Two years later, another blow—
this one to Andrew's forehead
and he fell unconscious—
I hope—
into our river and drowned.
Three weeks of memories is now
too short.
I wish for more. I grieve
even for the bad times.
Sorrow has burned
the skin from my face.
Tears are scalding water
on raw eyes and cheeks.
I remember the burned little girl
and the boy behind the blinds.
Now Andrew and I are the mother and child
in the corridor.
Sometimes I go outside to cry.
There by the river
a breeze pushes the hair off my forehead,
dries the tears on my cheeks,
rounds its mouth
and blows on the wound
around the steel pin through my chest.

My Husband

My husband's garden is in its second bloom.
He has planted all of the front yard
leaving narrow grass paths for me to wander.
I'll find him somewhere in the maze,
in the rose bed, the tea garden,
or the biblical herbs.
He is there fingering the amaranthus,
"love lies bleeding." He is a surgeon.
"A carpenter," he says,
"just nailing bones back together."
I've seen him move his hands
up a stranger's arm
from wrist to elbow to shoulder,
asking "Does this hurt?
Does this hurt? Where is your pain?"
When I find him, I put his hand
over my heart and tell him, "I hurt here."
"I know," he says. His son drowned
three weeks before I met him.
He kneels in the garden.
The sun is a white radiance on his back.
He picks a bouquet of leaves,
gives me an offering of aroma,
his hands cupped
as though I were to drink.
He says, "I'm growing teas for you,
chamomile and mint and hibiscus.
You can sip it
through a candied angelica straw.
And there's feverfew for your headaches
and comfrey for your bones;

and for your general welfare,
I'm growing sage.
It was sacred in Roman times,
harvested by one ceremonially washed,
barefoot, wearing a white tunic.
It could be gathered
only after offering a sacrifice."

In the Taxi

The driver never stopped talking,
told us
he had been mugged
so he had a revolver
in the car.
But it wasn't thugs
he worried about,
it was drunk drivers
like the one that killed
his son.
He had quit his old job.
"Couldn't concentrate," he said.
Was driving eighteen hours a day.
"Can't sleep," he said.
He talked the whole time.
Said he didn't know
what to say to his wife.
He left us at our door
to drive all night
through the empty city streets.
We walked down our long, dark hall
past the pictures of our two dead boys
knowing how far he had to go.

Foxes

How forlorn they looked,
the two red foxes dangling over the hanger,
sold separately
at the vintage clothing store sale.
They were whole bodies—
heads, legs, tails, even claws,
everything but one severed paw.
My friend giggled
as I wrapped one,
then both around my neck.
They seemed alive
chasing each other around my shoulders.
They were warm
nuzzling against my ears.
Sold—the pair.

To celebrate their rescue
I wore them to tea
with my brother
at the new cafe nearby.
He said the woman at the register
grimaced when we walked in,
the foxes and I.
"No."
"Yes, I'm certain," he said.
I gently laid them down together
by my side in the booth.
A waitress brought a menu:

vegetarian Rueben, tofu cheesecake,
filtered pure water, no smoking.
"Oh no."

Does this woman think
I could have killed these babies next to me?
I would have opened the trap,
freed them.
Does anyone think it was my fault—
Andrew drowning?
I wasn't there
to free him from the river
and carry him back to the house
as I carry these two little ones
in my arms
out of the restaurant and home.

The Dance

My life is a circle
forever going forward,
forever coming back.
His birth, his death,
my birth, my death,
ad infinitum.
Is not the symbol for infinity
a circle twisted over itself
in the middle, forever
squeezed in agony? Is that
the wringing out of sorrow?
Grief runs on a circular track.
When pain strikes us
at any point on the line,
we go fully around again
like a sleek greyhound
who will never catch
the mechanical rabbit.
Will the golden ring
free us from sorrow?
We kill ourselves
chasing foolishness
in revolving doors.
My child was only playing.
The river that took him
has never spoken,
the ever-widening concentric circles
that marked his fall
silently backed away.
Tell me, are life and death

a hoop flipped over,
one side like the other?
Life is a closed circuit;
blood flows back to the heart.
The solar system spins in circles.
Am I a dancing pirouette,
heart pounding with each revolution,
eyes seizing the same spot—his grave,
my reference point for balance,
arms swirling over my head
stirring heaven's stars
with a circular motion,
grasping for an imaginary cord,
my calloused, pointed toe
drilling into the ground beneath me,
my grave spiraling below?

Your Questions

I'll tell you;
I'll be bold.
You cannot know what this is like.
I don't want you to know
firsthand. But do not dare surmise
or worse, pass judgment—
you'll hear a different poem from me.
Not the poem that tries
with constricted throat
to speak the unspeakable,
recapture in foolish, shallow syllables
the trauma of loss
so you might
know for a moment
grief that gives life,
transcends,
blesses with wisdom.
It's my choice to share these lessons.
It's your choice to not listen
if you cannot bear
what I also thought
I could not survive.
I will understand
and wait
until you need this lesson
like a lifeline
when you are drowning.
You will die, too, you know.
There's nothing I can do about it
but have you drown in my poem
for only a moment,
then come gulping to the surface
looking into my eyes

smiling because you are not dead
but happier than you were before
to shake the water off your head,
go home and kiss your children,
tuck them in bed,
sleep yourself unsettled
but wake somehow refreshed.
So I keep telling my story,
what I know to be true.

I am different.
I felt it right away.
I wanted to die to be
with Andrew.
Others knew;
some forced themselves to touch me
as though my flesh *had* fallen away,
leaving my skull
to remind everyone of death.
It has taken me years
to recognize my face in the mirror,
to know who I am,
but I tell you
my face shines like Moses' face
and I refuse to hide it anymore,
cover it with makeup
or put on a smile

to make it easier for you.
Do not avoid my eyes.
Do not walk away from me.
I am a mother.
Come close, sit down
and listen.

We'll begin with your questions.
Ask me, for example,
why you never received a thank-you note
for flowers, food
or charity contributions
because I need to tell you.
After the funeral, I threw away
the funeral home's inadequate
thank-you notes given to me in a box.
I intended to write all of you,
but years went by,
and I never thanked you
for salvation in flowers,
nourishment of fried chicken,
poetry in "Given in memory of . . .."
One day I hope to see
the Jerusalem pine a friend planted in Israel,
Andrew's oak pew in a new chapel by the beach,
a music room full of children singing
where his memorial plaque proclaims:
"Make a joyful noise."
When my knees buckled,
I fell backward
onto your gifts like pillows
and like a person convalescing

propped them around me.
Now that I am better I can
write a long note to say thank you
and I love you
and I'm sorry it all happened.

For words of comfort even now,
you might say and some did say,
"You still have another son."
Now I ask you,
"Do you hear
your logic?
When your mother died
did your living father make it easier?"
What saved you, you ask?
Unconditional love.
I was lucky with Andrew.
We were happy.
Nothing left undone.
Our last moments together were filled
with laughter. Pushing him in his tire swing
by the river,
he was curled inside the circle
like a baby in the womb,
giggling
because he knew at random
I would catch him,
hold him close to my heart,
unwilling to let go,
and cover his face with kisses.
Fill your relationships
with all the photos in your mind
until they are so good

you will be afraid of losing them, and you will.
But that will not kill you,
you'll survive and live on.
It's regret that destroys you,
anything left undone.
You see I tell you
what you already know.
Don't shake your head
and dismiss this because it is simple.

Let's pretend you have climbed
a dangerous mountain,
reached the summit to see
the wise old woman who lives on the peak.
Your bruised knuckles knock on her door.
It opens. She's standing there—
you can't believe it—
wearing shorts,
her hair pulled back in a rubber band.
You've come all this way,
it's not what you expected
and worse yet
she goes to her desk,
gives you a paper,
one of hundreds, all typed,
"Live each day as though it were your last."

You see our problem,
you already have this at home
in a needlework picture.
Because it is nothing new
you may turn away,

but I won't worry about you.
You are a climber,
an asker of questions
with answers
cross-stitched on your walls at home,
hung in old frames on a nail,
hiding a flaw in the plaster.

I'll ask the next question for you
because you may not think to wonder,
"Is there anything you would have done differently?"
Yes, I'd bring his body home,
put his blue casket in my living room,
group all the flowers around him.
Imagine all the flowers.
Think of two more days
for me to look at my child,
discover the bruise
on his forehead that wasn't there
when we were playing.
I learned of his injury
weeks later
when the funeral director told me,
"He was so beautiful.
We did nothing but cover the blow."
For two more days
I could have spoken to my child face to face
before forced to speak
only to darkness or you.
There were not enough chances
to touch him,

put my cheek next to his.
I wouldn't have been afraid
of my child's body;
but I left him at the funeral home
in the corner room
on the second floor
and visited whenever I could
because I did not want to scare you.

Next time will be different.
I'll put my loved one in the house
like my mother's family used to do,
and we'll all gather around
like sitting by a fire.
At the cemetery, like a rabbi
I'll take the shovel
and heap the dirt back in the hole,
do the raking and sodding myself.

Let me tell you.
You would not know to ask
about the day they set his tombstone.
I watched them stand the small granite cross
in a footing of wet cement.
When the workers left,
I touched the stone
carved with his name in full
because that's the way he said it,
written in all capitals
because that's the way he wrote it:
ANDREW CAMERON MINTON.
I broke a branch
so I could write to my child

in the margin of wet cement,
"I love you. I miss you.
Thank God I will see you again."
You see I have learned
chances don't come again.
I listen when they say,
"Opportunity is brief.
Remember cement gets hard.
Yesterday is set concrete
unable to record your words."

Shall we go on? I have seven years to tell you.
I read the next question in your eyes:
"How have you managed to go on?"
You'll hate my answer:
more needlework,
perhaps a needlepoint pillow?
Let me paint
the canvas for you.
Now go home with your fists
full of rainbows of wool,
thread the needle yourself,
strain to see
through your tears,
pull each thread through the holes,
in and out like a pulse.
Nail your finished canvas on a frame,
stretch it square,
bind it with cord

braided of your hair.
Put it on your sofa, show it to your friends,
teach them *One Day At a Time.*

No more questions, but you are concerned.
You suggest I get out and get some exercise.
Exercise!? Exercise!?
Grief is isometric.
Are you looking at my face?
I have the face of a sprinter.
I grimace and strain
like the runners I saw
in the New York marathon.
Those toward the end were suffering,
dying, though more alive than most of us
cheering for people we didn't know,
"Don't give up! Keep going!"
Some were passing them water.
The runners ran on, some fell skinning their knees.
If you pass me a cup of water
you will see
what I see up the road—
a rugged uphill course I'm determined to finish.
I'll make it
if I pace myself,
forgive myself when I fall,
and stop long enough to accept the water you offer.

Thirteenth Birthday

September 29, 1991.
He would have been thirteen today.
There will be no party for my teenager.
There is work to do in the yard.
I'll cut off the arms of ivy
reaching toward the river.
Their begging will not persuade
him to come back.
I'll prune dead roses,
lay them in circles
like memorial wreaths
on the grave-like mound of compost.
Using my heavy metal rake,
I'll comb pine needles
out of the lawn like tangles
out of wet hair. I'll pour
grass seed into a small blue cart,
walk back and forth slowly
as though strolling a baby carriage.
I'll turn on the sprinkler to soak the seeds,
stand back and watch it oscillate
back and forth by the bulkhead,
waving goodbye to sorrow.
That will encourage me to do what I must
in the attic—sort through the last
of his clothes. Over my head on the roof,
I know fall leaves are piling
one upon another like children at recess;
that I neither hear nor see them
does not mean they are not there.

To My Parents

July 26 again,
eighth anniversary of his death.
On the road to my parents' home
old trees hang over the narrow road
like grown-ups over a crib.
White Queen Anne's lace
ruffle the roadside like eyelet curtains
at an open nursery window.
The fields are fertile,
crops green.
Summer is pregnant again.

There are no babies
in our family anymore.
I am going home alone.
No boys, no toys, no luggage.
I arrive empty-handed
except for my nightgown.
Peach gladioli in my grandmother's glass pitcher
greet me at the door.
My father grows them for my mother
to cut and bring inside
on occasions like today.
The kitchen is full of fresh fruit
and pineapple brownies.
Sunshine, an ocean
breeze and clean sheets
are in my bedroom.
The crib is gone.

For years it was hard for me
to visit here;

my sorrow too great
to carry up the stairs.
As though I were an invalid,
my parents would help me through
the door. "Is there anything
we can carry for you?"
    "I wish," I would say.
"Is there anything we can
fix for you?"
    "I wish," I would say.
"Is there anything we can
get for you?"
    "I wish," I would say.

They live without their youngest grandson,
but how do they live with me?
At night, I go into their bedroom
as I did as their little girl.
They lie in bed, their glasses
folded on their nightstands
like their arms across their chests.
What must I look like to them
without their glasses,
without their grandchild?
Their blue eyes gaze at me.
Their faith looks forward
to seeing their grandson.
Compassion and wisdom
are written on their foreheads
like lines of a poem
or names on a tombstone.
These last eight years

lie in wrinkles under their necks,
around their elbows,
across each knuckle.
I bend over them to kiss
the inscriptions on their foreheads
and pull the white spread up
over their beautiful bodies.
The role of parent or child
in our family
is as fluid as the river
that killed one of us.
It is how
we have survived.

Driving

You know how it is when you are driving:
suddenly you realize you've driven several miles,
but you don't remember getting there.
With grief the miles are years.
Driving is habit. The destination changes;
you are to turn left, but you still turn right.
When the child in the store calls, "Mom!"
I turn the way I always did.
We detour to avoid obstacles.
I drive blocks out of my way to bypass his playground.
If you are old enough, you will see
a car like one you owned when you were young,
and you will travel back through time.
Yesterday, I saw my child
in the passenger seat of a small car
approaching a red light. I changed
lanes to get a better look.
His head was the same, his blue eyes familiar.
He was close,
but his mother drove him away.
I should have driven forward, but I couldn't.
Wiping my eyes, I could see in my rear-view mirror
the driver behind me honking his horn, screaming,
"What's the matter with you?" The question
I was asking myself.

A Happy Poem

Thomas asks, "Why
don't you write a happy poem?
Can you write one about your rose garden?"
Because of Thomas, I won't say
the garden is the size and shape
of our family plot at the cemetery
or that the metal markers
resemble grey granite tombstones,
the roses' names in all capitals.
My son is right. I'll change
the names of the roses to suit myself
and this poem.
The white ones will become
Baby Powder, Tooth Fairy, and Christening Gown,
the pink ones:
First Word, First Step, First Grade,
the yellow:
Golden School Bus, Blond Beauty, and Baby Cup,
the lavender:
Blue Jeans, His Eyes, and Brother,
the three velvety red ones:
(soft as a newborn's face)
Love, Forever, Mom.
I'll rip out the cold metal markers,
replace them with my boys' Little Golden Books,
write a rose's new name on each title page
and for Thomas only happy-ending stories.
I'll border the roses with alphabet blocks
spelling out prayers and writing poems.
At the entrance to the garden,
I'll build an arch cascaded with fragrance
thanks to the carefree everblooming climber.
I'll invite strangers

to walk through the liquid aroma,
to dangle their feet in my fountain of youth.
I'll ask them to stretch out their hands,
touch the petals
like Adam reaching for the finger of God.
As I move through the beautiful roses
the thorns grab at the hem of my skirt,
first on one side, then the other
like my boys when we walked through a crowd.
I'll gather a bouquet as large as a baby,
cradle the flowers in my arms to the house.
I'll strip the stems
of thorns and lower leaves
then plunge them up to their necks
in warm water
as though giving them a bath.
I'll carry the huge bouquet upstairs to Thomas,
place it in front of the window in his room.
I'll leave a small white card signed MOM
with two eyes and a smile in the O.
And the thorns—I'll keep
in a closed silver box
beside the pictures of my boys by my bed.

Crazy

My friend's mother
died at eighty-five.
Lovingly, he tells stories
about her losing her mind.
He says it was odd toward the end
to visit and find notes
for her husband
pinned to her silk lampshades.
His father had been dead for years.
His mother would complain that at lunch
her old friend
(also years dead)
had not even looked up
when she called her by name.
Some evenings she entertained her parents,
always had to ask them to leave early
because her husband was coming home.
He was tired when he worked late.
She had to turn his bed back,
lay out his favorite pajamas,
be ready when he arrived.
I want to but don't do all of these things.

What If?

What if the divers had surfaced empty-handed?
What if someone had found him just sitting in a tree
mesmerized by the neighbors' small boats
passing back and forth in the water.
He would have been wide-eyed watching the flurry of lights.
Boats' red, green, and white running lights twinkled,
glittered like a magical, floating carousel.
He would have loved the flashlights of those on the shore
shining in all directions like gleaming swords.
He would never have forgotten
the blue lights on the police cars swirling
like the moonlit wake of the rescue boat.
The boat's searchlights and acrobatic divers
would seem to any child a circus act.
Had he jumped from the tree and come running,
the search would have been no more than a midnight cruise,
the black hearse would not have come for his body,
the helicopter pilot could have killed his floodlight,
the media would have abandoned their story,
and his grandmother never learned
from the eleven o'clock news
that her youngest grandson was missing from our yard.
Embracing him, would I have scolded him or covered him
with kisses of sweet relief? Definitely kisses,
probably never would have scolded him again at all.
Would I have let him sleep with me?
He asked to every night at bedtime.
No, that was not his place.
His room was across the hall where I could see him.
But he did drown and he is not in his room anymore.
Since that evening when he did not come when I called,
every night—he is in bed with me.

Underwater

This is holy ground.
Barefoot
I walk in my yard.
Some expected me to move.
A realtor called offering her services.
But I have stayed.
My fingernails have grown long.
My hair has silvered.
The boxwood hedge is as tall
as my son would be.
It was small plants
with leaves tiny as freckles
when I spaced and planted them years ago.
Our house is the same,
but the air outside is changed,
the atmosphere liquid,
as though the river has risen
over the bulkhead
and our yard has drowned.
Birds swim by overhead.
I see everything through a wet lens—
some call it baptism by submersion,
others call it tears.

My Work

It's a beautiful day, but I am depressed.
My mother says, "Don't just sit there,
do something constructive." She would vacuum.
I'll do laundry. I'll gather my poems—
those too tear-stained
and sticky with sentimentality—
and wash them. I'll collect them
in the pouch of my apron,
carry them to the river
like a mother kangaroo
taking her baby for a bath.
I'll use the bulkhead for a washboard,
scrape the pages up and down,
watch the sorrow wash away,
then hang them on the line.
They will flap in the wind
like white surrender flags.
I'll give up
the idea of loss,
wait for them to dry,
take them down,
and count them like blessings.
The one about Andrew's death
I'll fold into a white hat
to wear on my head
like a nurse
who knows the secrets of healing.
The ones about Thomas
will become boats with white sails.
I'll send them up river,
commission the expedition
to discover his new world.
With scissors I'll cut folded poems

the way I taught my boys to make snowflakes.
I'll sew together cutwork squares,
making panels for the dining room windows
like old lace curtains.
For a tablecloth,
I'll starch and iron long ones
and invite my mother for tea.
I'll spread honey and nuts
between the thin, crisp pages
like baklava
and serve the delicacy to her
on white paper plates.
We'll use the washed poems for napkins
to wipe crumbs from the corners of our mouths
and tears from our cheeks
because we'll cry.
We always do.
But the sun will shine
through the cutwork at the window,
casting delicate shadows
on white plaster walls
like handwriting around the room.
When she leaves she will take
a painting of flowers on a poem
I've worked on all night
just to get it right.
I'll stand at the door waving a poem
like my grandmother's monogrammed handkerchief
until my mother is out of sight down the lane.
Then I'll go to my bedroom,
make the shortest poems into small pillowcases,
sew ruffles on the hems and stuff them

with the boys' old baby pillows.
I'll prop them behind me and around me
and write thank-you notes and love letters.
I'll send a letter, not a poem,
to Thomas away at school.
I'll write to the father of the boys
and thank him for such beautiful children.
I'll draw my father a funny picture
because he cannot bear to read my poems.
And tonight, I'll write something private.
I'll perfume it, fold it,
slide it under my husband's pillow,
then lie down on the clean white sheets
waiting for him to come home.

The Dinner Party

The sun squints curiously
behind eyelids of clouds
to watch me string the dogwood
with white Christmas lights.
I swim through the spider webs
hanging off each limb.
The webbed shroud has covered
the tree all summer,
its delicate silver cords
grasp the white roses
that weep and fall
over the stone wall.
The tide comes in
to see my foolishness,
asks with its chin
on the bulkhead,
"Christmas lights in August?"
Company is coming for dinner.
We will eat outside
under the tree,
clink our glasses
like a bell choir.
The cicadas will accompany us
with shrill rattles
as they escape
the brittle molds of themselves,
leaving exact likenesses
on the trunk of the tree.
I will ask my young guests
about their babies and toddlers.
They will tell me they never knew

they could love so much
and know so little.
I'll tell them
to have at least four children
and quote my grandmother
who would say,
"You are eating your white bread and butter."
It will be Christmas
under the illuminated tree.
They will give me gifts
of beautifully wrapped stories
containing small children,
huge hearts,
fragile futures.
When they leave,
I will kiss each one
in case I never see them again.
I'll leave the lights on all night.
The next day, I will clear the table
and the spider webs
that return during the night.
I'll collect the empty cicada shells,
line them up on the table where we dined—
a little cicada parade—
the way my children did when they were small
and lived here. One story
I keep for myself.

I Thirst

I'd give anything
for a cup of the joy
my child gave me.
Never mind the daily bread.
Now I am creator
molding and remolding
every new and old love in my life
with prayer, edification,
risks and kisses
to recreate what I had with Andrew.
Fear of loss
and walls of self-protection
will kill me
long before a broken heart.
I pray,
let every death
break me so.

The Andrew Poems is the winner of the 1992 first-book competition in the TTUP Poetry Award Series. The competition was supported generously by The CH Foundation and the Helen Jones Foundation in honor of the sisters Christine DeVitt and Helen DeVitt Jones.